Her Soul Uncovered

poems

NISHA JARIWALLA

ISBN Ebook: 979-8-218-69192-9
ISBN Paperback: 979-8-218-69193-6

In memory of my beloved father

Raxit Jariwalla

To my beloved mother and brother

Sonal Jariwalla

Neil Jariwalla

Unveiling the depths of grief and uncertainty, *Her Soul Uncovered* invites the reader to walk alongside the author to uncover a path of healing and self-discovery, bringing about hope and renewal. I hope this collection provides a safe space and a comforting reminder that you carry more strength than you realize and are never truly alone.

May you find solace here.

Grieving   *1*

Becoming   *43*

Grieving

I was nineteen
when our hands embraced for the last-
only to part too soon
now but a memory of the past

For all I ever long for
is to travel back
relive all the memories
the two of us had

And wait till a time
when I could bear the sad,
than go through the pain
of losing a love ever-last

At nineteen
with so much innocence to be had
all I am trying to say is
I miss you, Dad

I long for the day when our hands embrace again
Reunited somewhere amidst the skies of heaven

The little girl stood beside him at the temple altar
her father standing tall gazing down at his daughter
he placed her hands on top of his, in devout prayer
steady and strong, as they bowed their heads down together

Years later at the same temple altar
I am older and grown, and my hands do not falter
for I still feel your hands with mine, steady but stronger
offering a prayer to God, like father like daughter

...as if you never left, and I never lost

Not having the chance to share goodbyes
brought comfort to my soul
because that meant I would see you again
if not in this lifetime, then in the next

...it was never goodbye

You told me
to become something
little did I know
those words would be your last
echoing so deeply in my ear
leaving an eternal imprint on my chest
feeding my only impetus in life to honor them
and ring them true

Now that I have become something
you always wished for me to do
I desperately wish I could have shared it with you

...I wish you were still here

I still see you in my *dreams*
us walking hand in hand
only me holding yours a little tighter
hugging you a little stronger
forcing my eyes shut a little longer
before I knew I couldn't *dream forever*

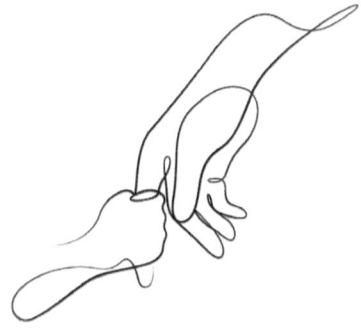

I came to realize that your love
was God's love in human form
and when you left this physical body
your love never left, and your soul never died
but continued on with mine
...existing in another dimension in time

I apologize to my younger self
for trying to relate to the trivial conversations I once knew
for molding myself into a world I could no longer identify with
a world I no longer knew
I could not relate to them talking about the gossip next door
when I was fearful
if I would even survive another day more
without you
I apologize to my younger self
that the worry I had to carry
was mine to bear so heavy
at 19 years of age
when all I should have known was innocence

...the loss of naivety

Wherever you are in this universe
and wherever your soul takes you
I hope you are happy and free
and I hope somewhere in your celestial travels
amidst the clouds in the heavenly skies
you still think of me

...that we are still father and daughter in another universe

Mother,
you consoled me in your arms
after losing the love of your life
carried my pain as if it were your own
even with so much heartache to bear
you didn't show it
but it was undeniably there
your love knows no bounds
your strength, nothing compares

When your burden is too heavy to bear
please do not hesitant to share it with me
I would more than gladly
lighten your load
as you have mine all these years

...your pain is my pain

I saw the girl in front of me shedding tears
her hands buried in her face weeping
crouched down in a state of full despair
fearful of uncertainty running rampant in the air

I spoke kind words
words that she wanted to hear
of how beautiful she looked with smeared makeup
how brave she was to face her fears

She glanced at me and offered a smile
I smiled back at her, and decided to stay a while
pulled her hair back, wiped her tears with my hands
saw a familiar face of beauty behind her dark brown bangs

Only that girl was me
offering solace to the very girl
who told herself day in and day out
that her reflection was beautiful

...it was me in the mirror

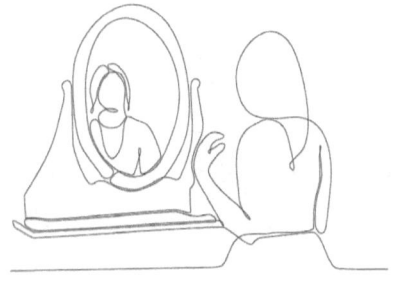

The grief you carry holds no timeline
the healing after dark knows no finish line
your experiences are your own, to be felt and lived
without external judgement of your pain within
do not let the world tell you what to feel
when to "get over it" and when to heal
they are not you, do not make them so
you owe it to yourself to go with your flow
and feel what you feel until it hurts no more
for you have been through so much more
than what the people say next door

...it is your life and your life only

Those feelings you feel
are not foreign to you
please do not undermine yourself
and act like a foreigner in the land of heartache
as if the tides will not bring you back to shore
stronger than ever
you are not a foreigner to this land
you have been here many times before

...act like it

When I felt deep sadness in my heart
I realized the only arms I needed
were those of my own
tightly hugging my body
and my soul whispering *"you are all I need"*

On some days, I wish I could *unlearn* all the lessons
if that meant I could *spare myself* one less day of heartache

Just as happiness is fleeting
so too is pain
but why are we so hard on ourselves
thinking *the pain will never leave*
my dear, no matter what happens in this lifetime
one truth is knowing
...that everything leaves

All the times she struggled
she reminded herself
she could fall back on
the previous hurdles she had overcome
but the very first time rock bottom hit
she had no compass
but simply entrusted herself to God
and His greater purpose

The girl stood at the train tracks, luggage in hand
waiting for the next train embarking to a new land
but the train flew past, full speed ahead
she wept inconsolably, for she missed her chance
but the wheels kept turning, not daring to look back
to see the girl in desperation chasing a wrong path
the right train was yet to come
and when it came at last
the doors welcomed her with open arms
a goodbye to the past
for her destination was far greater than she had ever imagined
for nothing could stop God's divine intervention

...she deserved so much more than what she begged for

The tears did not roll down
but there was a sadness in her eyes
whilst she talked about life
carrying it all inside

...the weight of a broken heart

The only permanence I will ever know in this life is
...*impermanence*

I wish your actions showed
what your eyes spoke
maybe then I would not have felt
that this connection was
unrequited

You walked into my life like it was everything
tested the waters to get your bearings
stayed a while to exchange pleasantries
and left like it was nothing
only to leave me stranded helplessly
I guess that was destiny
that you came and left so suddenly
do not come back daringly
for I will no longer be
your temporary remedy

Even though the mind knew what it had to do
the heart helplessly stayed a little while longer
whilst breaking in two

Just because I didn't say it
and you didn't show it
doesn't mean
we didn't feel it

My younger self
called out to my older self
crying out
why is the narrative always
I am not worthy of them
instead of
They are not worthy of me
my older self replied
do not worry my child
so much of life will happen *for you*
that the narrative will become
I am worthy of all the abundance
that whether they come and go
leave or stay
my heart would not falter either way

...I am living proof of it everyday

Your worthiness is not to be played
like a puppet on a string
casually tossed around
by others on a whim
without free will at your own very hands
your worth is fully inherent and innate
do not let this world consume you and create
an unworthy girl with no sense of self worth
hopelessly fallen to the hands of this karmic earth
you have been born to fly and conquer with endless wings
than to be held down like a puppet on strings

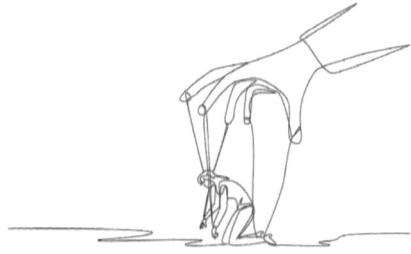

There was never such a thing as *you and me*
only forever an illusion in our minds
of something *never meant to be*

It takes a different kind of strength
to gracefully let go of everything
you thought was yours, but never was

If love is unconditional
why does it take so long to invite itself in
I have been waiting and longing
but my patience has grown thin
for a love to enter my heartspace
nourish me from the roots down
yet everytime it comes knocking
it suddenly turns back around
that I find myself sitting here
pondering in deep thought
will the right love ever come
will it find where to knock?
when the birds start humming in song
the love that is for you will come in due time
one that will pull on your heartstrings just right
but until that times comes the days will feel like a chore
while I hopelessly wilt- another day more

...waiting for that unconditional love to come knocking at my door

The sun shone so effortlessly upon you
wherever we went it followed
but every time we had to part
the sun came undone, your shadow dark
little did I know
I was the sun all along
casting its rays upon you
making you real
but you were not...

...I made you special

Loving me more did not mean
it would not be hard to walk away
but knowing it would be, and still choosing myself

You have never met me
yet you claim to know everything about me
the good and bad
the past and present
the rumors and secrets that run free
so then tell me
tell me
how I walked in those ragged shoes along rugged lands
picked up the weight of a broken heart with bare hands
stayed afloat while fighting demons drowning my mind
how I learned to endure this destined path of my life
while you were busy conjecturing it on the sidelines

So then tell me
tell me

If you claim to know everything about me...
...when you really know nothing about me at all

She spent all her days daydreaming
of everything that *could be*
losing the moment of the here and now
for her eyes were blind to see
all the miracles surrounding her
now in her reality
miracles that once upon a time she prayed for
yet she still craved and yearned for more

...material dissatisfaction

Sometimes it is okay to let
the natural *tide* of the *ocean* take control
if staying afloat is too hard
do not be afraid to *sink* a little
we must be willing to surrender
to the raw *depth* of our emotions
the rooted essence of pain
our truest vulnerability
before rising to the *surface*
renewed and revived
ready to take another *breath*
to conquer this karmic ocean of life

...let yourself go with the flow

Though she was struggling
she chose to look forward
towards the path ahead of her
for even though she could not see it yet
the happiest, most healed version of her
was yet to come
and that girl did not deserve
to be given up on

The weight on her chest felt insurmountable
like a pile of heavy bricks, though already crumbled
yet she carried the weight through shifting sands
tried to find balance through unfamiliar lands

When finally she decided to surrender and fall
and suddenly God took the weight of it all
in His hands and said My child listen to me
all the burden upon you so heavy
was never only yours to carry

...Surrender unto Me, and I will take care of thee

I realized
I placed my worth in you
something external to me
because I loved you

But I had to let go
free myself of you
and remember who I was
before I met you

When I find my way back
it will be a testament to
the inner strength I found
to finally bid you adieu

Never again
for I have learned my lesson to
never lose my worth
and misplace it in you

That image you drew
looked nothing like me
I saw no resemblance
of the portrait before me

Of course, how could I
when your perception of me
arose from a life you never lived
far from my reality

...your perception of me is not me

Grief remains but an indelible imprint on my heart
like a turmeric stain smeared on my white cotton shirt
surpassing the passage of time
infinite and one of a kind

Years later
I pull out that white shirt from my closet
it's signature yellow stain, just as when I had worn it
grown fainter, nearly blended into the stark white
as if it belonged there all this time

A part of me
a part of my childhood
with turmeric-stained hands reminding me
that grief will fade but always remain
imprinted on my heart, forever to stay

...like a turmeric stain that just never washes away

You must know
the story of your life is not over
when *one chapter of your book ends*
your life is a series of new beginnings
waiting to unfold
if you turn the page
to the *next chapter God sends*

Becoming

I looked up to see
another treacherous mountain before me
yearning to be climbed
to unveil its breathtaking story

I glanced back
at the mountaintops in hindsight
once so unattainable
now envisioned with familiar eyes

I finally decided to let go and admire
the beauty of the here and now, a moment to surrender
to the view I longed to attain, many mountains ago
existing right before me, yet I was blind to my growth

With fresh eyes I could now clearly see
that very mountain standing before me, *was me*
for there were vast fields and no mountains to climb
just me holding myself back all this time

...the very mountain was me

I realized the transformation within myself
when my definition of happiness did not lie
within a person, place, or thing
but within the core of my being and my relationship with God
a feeling of peace I could resonate with
anywhere, any time, any place
a part of me that could never be replaced, lost, or taken

...such as a person, place, or thing

Just because your eyes could not envision
the sun peeking behind the clouds
the faint rainbow appearing after the rain
the shine hidden behind the tainted glass of steel
does not mean the light amidst the dark
did not exist

For when the time is right
and when the stars align
will the light shine through
in due course of time

...there will always be light after dark

When my hands let go
God held them
walked me down the road less traveled
hand in hand
to a new destiny I couldn't yet see
but one He had orchestrated all along
for me

The rainbow is still the rainbow
even if one day it appears faint
and another day bright
for every time it appears
after a season of tears
every spectrum of color comes to light
for it still fights to shine fully, every shade in sight
no matter how fierce the rain in the skies

The endless pool of tears shedding from her eyes
grew a beautiful garden
cultivated of roses without thorns
leaves renewed, without wilt
trees sturdy and tall, without sway
a garden full of sunshine without gray

A garden so fierce and untamed
that even as less tears shed
it grew magnificent flower beds
of sunflowers reaching their utmost heights
for she was unstoppable
despite the tears in her eyes

...you can heal and grow at the same time

I used to hold on so tightly to things
which no longer served me
and later found that while loosening my grip
my hands seamlessly outstretched to things
which resonated with my being and aligned with my soul

She learned to *fall in love with*
how she stumbled and how she flew
how she hurt and how she grew
cherishing all the struggles
birthing lessons to use
to pick herself up
and start anew

And somewhere along the journey
in the process of becoming
she undeniably
fell in love with herself...too

I didn't realize
that letting go of you
meant also shedding
the past version of me
who longed for you

So I guess in the end
healing meant
letting go of you...
and letting go of me...too

When you find yourself in a place of suffering,
think 'how lucky am I to be molded again and again
only to become an even stronger version of me'

...perspective is everything

If one day you decide to let her go
just know she did everything she could to stay
so one day when you realize she was your greatest loss
just know it will be too little too late

The love between you and me
was a love never meant to be attained
proven
nurtured
or embellished
but a love that simply existed
beyond the realm of the tangible
within the time and space of you and me
a love untouched, but eternal
unspoken, yet felt
unburdened by the human need to prove it
a love that awakened
when our souls crossed paths one day
and recognized one another
and that was simply enough
for it to exist

When you pulled yourself out of suffering
and the healing had begun
you started anew with revived hopes for the future
for you became the sun

but before the light shone through
when this karmic world hardened you
molding you into someone you are not
you forget you were the sun
amidst your shadow of doubt

but your light is always there
even if it grows fainter amidst the gray
as the sun will always come again
you will always rise, even on your darkest days

It is a sad truth
that the wiser we become in this life
the greater amount of innocence we leave behind
if I could choose how my destiny unraveled
I would have *held on* to all the innocence
and *let go* of all the lessons

The fierce gust of winds picked up yet again
but the butterfly remained relentless in spreading its wings
so tenacious that even the force of mother earth
could not convince it to surrender
...invincible

I think the most beautiful thing you can do
is feel your deepest feelings
even when it is hard to surrender
to *vulnerability*
for that is what makes us human
yet the world has taught us to repress emotion
kept trapped in a jar
yearning to be opened
thereby perpetuating the human condition
of pain, distress, and affliction

Oh how I wish
I could fast forward in time
to envision that everything turned out just fine
but then maybe we wouldn't find the need to try
to discover ourselves and fight the battles we fight
our journey is so much more than the finish line
it's a culmination of experiences yearning to be tried
please allow yourself to let go of what might
and lean into this so-called adventure called *life*

I tried so hard to articulate
how much you meant to me
yet no words uttered from my mouth
you meant so much
I could not convey the magnanimity
of what your presence in my life
was to me
mother, you are simply...*extraordinary*

...thank you for being my everything

I wish I could hug the younger version of me
crouch down in front of her
place my hand over her heart
and whisper in her ear
that light shining brightly inside of you
you may lose it along the way
but it will always return after gray
do not be afraid
you will find again someday

for here I am, living once again
that same girl, reunited with that long lost light
still shining oh so bright
no matter how many years have passed her by

Dear little one frolicking in the grass,
I look at you
and all I hope for is
life protects your innocence for as long as it can
that the hurt doesn't ache
that the tears don't shed
for too long
because when reality comes knocking on your door
looming over you like an endless burden
shaking you to your core
you deserve to find yourself again
heal again
and frolick in the grass once again

with your resilient, beating heart
just as before

I wish you could look from up above
and watch the younger version of you
live, cry, learn, love, fall, grow, and heal
I wish you could see yourself through your eyes
than wait for the world to make you realize
how beautiful you truly are
you are inherently perfect
without the need to try
do not do yourself a disservice
to put on a disguise
just to be "beautiful"
for another pair of eyes
in this world full of lies
when your eyes alone
are enough to visualize
your authenticity

...the only approval you will ever need is that of your own

Beneath the surface, beyond the skin
burns a fire, fierce within
not just her beauty, nor a fleeting glance
but a spirit that dares to rise and dance

she has built her dreams with steady hands
carving her path through shifting sands
with every challenge, every fight
she proves her strength, she owns her light

beauty fades, but she remains
a mind unyielding, a heart untamed
so hear me now, and truly see—
she is more than just pretty

Her smile was one that magnified rooms she walked in
reaching the eyes, capturing the genuineness within
but little did she know that in all her strife
she would be fighting to bring that smile back to life

I hope the world brings light to her, I pray
takes away the pain and heartache she thought would remain
so that a smile once lost finds her eyes again someday
as if all the gray she ever knew was that of yesterday

We always find ourselves striving towards
'something great'
only to find that when the pursuit ends
we strive for the next
and the next...
didn't you believe that last great thing was the last great thing?

...maybe it is simply *the pursuit* that keeps us alive

If there ever comes a day
when we must part ways
just know
no passage of time
would my feelings fade
of loving you
forever and always

Maybe it is better it turned out this way
that our souls could dance freely
within the timespace of you and me
a space not too far out of reach
but not too close for hearts to bleed
a perfect *in between*
where you and me can still feel each other's
electricity
just enough spark to keep us coming back
only to keep us at arms length
this not so happy medium of push and pull
is what makes us crazy
but maybe all the mesmerization
would tire quickly
if we had one another readily
for our souls apart yet intertwined
dancing on a single thread
keeps the love alive and free till no end
maybe it is best this way
for you and me
were never meant to be
so let us love each other from a distance
for eternity

The truth is
there will never be a day I do not think of you
but the other truth is
there will never be a day more that I choose to lose myself
longing to be with you

when my eyes met yours for the first time
I felt a nostalgic sense of familiarity and belonging
as if our souls had intertwined in a previous lifetime
...only to be separated, and reunited in this

I knew you *were the one*
when our eyes met
and our hearts *beat as one*

I learned to embrace and to succumb
to the falling, hurting, and pain
which made me come undone
for it was necessary for what was yet to come
a new version of me who had fully become
little did I know
the place I started from
was just as beautiful
as the journey to overcome

...the process of becoming

The heart had to surrender and let go endlessly in this life
only to become so resilient
that eventually losing the world meant nothing
than losing its own beat, which meant everything

There will always come a time
when the autumn leaves shed
only to be renewed in spring
so too will come a time
when the old versions of ourselves shed
to uncover *what newness brings*

...we must shed to start anew

When I was young
I could not appreciate
the ability to know grief and loss
or see the beauty in pain

now that I am older and a little bit wiser
I realize how lucky I truly was
to live the human experience
at such a young age

for nothing in this life is ours
it withers away
to remain detached
is the ultimate gain

I have always admired those
who see pain as *abundant wealth*
as an opportunity to bloom from the hurt
growing into their most courageous selves
nurturing their new-found wisdom
and spreading it with the world

...pain is in fact a gift

Her heart was strung out but remained soft through it all
survived daggers and knives piercing its walls
yet she kept inviting pain in
as it knocked on her door
dived into the depths of heartache
even when she could bear no more
for she knew embracing pain with open arms
was far better than putting up walls
for the hurt would just linger on
letting the heart bleed
like a bird forever caged, yearning to be set free
so her heart remained soft and open
letting the pain and rough times pass
not letting the world change her
but changing the world
by remaining true to herself

To be balanced in happiness and distress
abundance and lack thereof
disharmony and harmony
is the true meaning of *being liberated*

This karmic cycle of birth and death
is inevitable
and *guaranteed*
unlike the sacred space existing
in between
this sacred space called life
where souls can run free
for a moment unharnessed
by this cyclical duality
of birth and death
for if this space is all we have
let us feed our souls deeply
and surrender to our spiritual calling
our truest divinity
than become entangled in material propensity
perpetuating this never-ending cycle
for eternity

I hope the more you endure in this life
the more resilient your heart becomes
the less burden your soul carries
and the less time it takes for you
to find yourself again

They say change is the only constant in life
but so too is the falling, grieving, healing, growing and rising
life is but an *endless cycle of becoming*

The thunder came furiously pounding on her door
she tried to resist
yet was met with more
God came down and spoke with force
"you've fought this storm many times before
do not resist, let it run its course"
she took her armor off, let the thunder roar
the storm came and went
as it did before
she stood speechless, yet finally at peace like never before
for she realized
she no longer had to fight anymore

Some people have to bear so much hurt
before *the one* comes along
the one who brings so much healing and joy
as if all the hurt of before is long gone
so at the end of the day
that hurt is not in vain
for it led me to you
and that fate, no words can explain

If our mouths lose the ability to speak
our hands lose the ability to embrace
the love between the two of us
will forever stay alive
for our eyes alone will speak volumes
of a love language
that no words or physical embrace could ever describe

Dear self,
I hope everything you became
was everything you ever wanted to achieve
but most of all,
I hope everything you became
is everything you ever wanted to be

Healing was the only thing that completely *engulfed* me
... and *revived* me all at once

I think it is so beautiful
that your smile still reaches your eyes
after all this time

I long for the day
when the healed version of me
and the healed version of you
finally meet
and grow together *authentically*

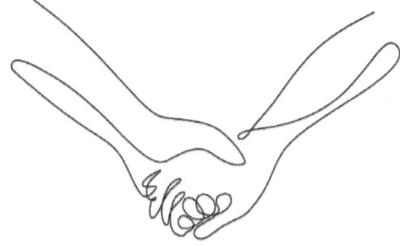

I hope you cultivate enough love for yourself
to gracefully turn the page
and open your heart fully
to the most abundant chapter of your life
that awaits just on the other side of
everything you have ever known

I simply cannot wait for the day
when you decide to finally live your life
for you
and only you

If I were to sit down and write
all the miracles God brought into my life
I would be writing for years on end
for every single day, in every small way
are countless of miracles He sends our way
we must be willing to uncover our eyes
to discover the miracles God sends in disguise
for my life has become so full and bright
seeing everything through the rays of God's loving light

The blank white canvas awaited me in the painting room
standing alone, without a soul in sight
but with a streak of daylight
shining directly upon it, as if inviting me in
at a closer glance stood a table setting perched next to it
adorned with cans of brushes, plump and exquisite
paint bottles unopened and new
mason jars filled with water clear as dew
I sat down and stared at the fresh slate before me
untouched, inviting colors to run free
my paintbrush gliding across the canvas effortlessly
as tears rolled down my cheeks
smearing the colors into a beautiful hue
tears of happiness, realizing
...*I could always start anew*

Her beauty is timeless
like a sunset coupled with a warm ocean breeze
like palm trees swaying amidst a summer night's dream
like a ray of sunlight peeking amongst tall redwood trees
she embodies her spirit without falter
her beauty unbeknownst to her
a soul ageless
a heart courageous
a girl fearless
a beauty forever timeless

When you nurture it
nurture it with your heart and soul
take the time to sit down and listen
to its inner wants and needs untold
for all the intuition you seek
it carries tenfold
awakening your truest calling
to cherish and behold
and when it needs comfort
embrace it with both arms and hold steady
this sacred vessel of life and home called your body

To the girl who lost herself yet found her way,

I hope you uncover
deep within your flesh
unrelenting strength
to ignite flames
burning bridges of fear and self doubt in your mind
and in place of it
carve stoned pathways so resilient
that even a thousand matches could not burn down
the walls you so extraordinarily overcome
for after all this time
you magically rise like a phoenix from the ashes
shaking the dust off your wings
flying to your heart's steady beat
a resilient being
conquering the world till no end

To the girl who found her way back home to herself
...may she never have to part with her, ever again

The inspiration behind this sacred collection of poems are my beloved parents, who remain a guiding light in my life. They represent pillars of strength, character, humility and unconditional love, making me the person I am today. I would be nowhere and no one without them.

My father embodied values of compassion, resilience, patience and virtue dedicating his life work to alternative medicine. His sudden passing awakened a harsh truth of uncertainty and impermanence in this human life. *Her Soul Uncovered* is an honorary tribute to him and a source of guidance, healing, and hope for those who have endured the depths of loss, heartache, and grief.

ABOUT THE AUTHOR

Nisha Jariwalla is a physician assistant living in the Bay area. She developed a passion for writing poetry at the age of 19 at which time she started her own collection. Over the years, she continued to feed her passion as inspiration came to her. She continues to enjoy writing and sharing her work at local readings in hopes of resonating with others who have known grief and loss.